D1162999

The Grimy, Gross
Unusual
History of the
Toilet

BY NEL YOMTOV

Content Consultant: Barbara Penner, PhD
Bartlett School of Architecture, UCL
London, England

CAPSTONE PRESS
a capstone imprint

Velocity is published by Capstone Press,
151 Good Counsel Drive, P.O. Box 669, Mankato, Minnesota 56002.
www.capstonepub.com

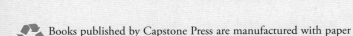

Books published by Capstone Press are manufactured with paper
containing at least 10 percent post-consumer waste.

Yomtov, Nelson.
  The grimy, gross, unusual history of the toilet/by Nel Yomtov.
    p. cm.—(Velocity. Unusual histories)
  Includes bibliographical references and index.
  Summary: "Traces the history of the invention of the toilet, from the earliest attempts
of ancient civilizations to the modern flush toilet design"—Provided by publisher.
  ISBN 978-1-4296-5489-0 (library binding)
  1. Toilets—History—Juvenile literature. 2. Eliminative behavior—History—Juvenile
literature. I. Title.
  TH6498.Y66 2012
  644'.6—dc22   2010049133

The author wishes to dedicate this book to his son, Jess.

Editorial Credits: Pam Mamsch
Art Director: Suzan Kadribasic
Designers: Deepika Verma, Jasmeen Kaur, Kanika Kohli

Photo Credits
Alamy: United Archives GmbH, 4 (bottom), David Lyons, 6, Oote Boe Photography, 7 (top), The Art
Archive, 7 (bottom), 35 (top), Art Directors & TRIP, 8, Roger Coulam, 15 (bottom), North Wind
Picture Archives, 16, Ivy Close Images, 18, Gabe Palmer, 19, Lordprice Collection, 21, 45 (middle),
The National Trust Photolibrary, 23 (top), Mary Evans Picture Library, 24 (bottom), Stephen Sykes,
25 (right), MARKA, 26-27, Frances Roberts, 31, Ambient Images Inc., 33 (bottom), Igor Kisselev,
36 (top left), PYMCA, 36 (right), Ei Katsumata, 39 (bottom right); Atech Flash Technology, Inc.: 29;
©2010 Arizona Board of Regents: 40; Bridgman Art Library: Andreas von Einsiedel/National Trust
Photographic Library/Saltram House, Devon, UK, cover, Agora Museum, Athens, Greece, 11 (top),
Ancient Art and Architecture Collection Ltd., 12, ©Look and Learn, 17 (bottom), Morgan,Evelyn De
(1855-1919)/©The De Morgan Centre, London, 37; Getty Images: John Macdougall/AFP, 5, Hulton
Archive, 10 (bottom), China Photos, 39 (top); Istockphoto: Bob Ingelhart, 1, 22, Pawe Strykowski,
11 (bottom), Felinda, 23 (bottom), Craig Cozart, 43 (bottom), Sarah Bossert, 44 (top); Jan Ctvrtnik/
Toilet Pages: 43 (top); Newscom: Philippe Maillard/akg-images, 9 (top), STR/Picture Alliance/dpa,
35 (bottom); NASA: 30; Photolibrary: Art Media, 13, 44 (bottom); Shutterstock: Shmeliova Natalia,
4 (back), Dan Breckwoldt, 9 (middle), Frank Bach, 9 (bottom), Alexwhite, 10 (top), Joseph Calev,
14 (top), Makhnach, 15 (compass rose), Phillip Minnis, 20 (bottom), Nyasha, 24-25, 45 (top),
Clearviewstock, 30 (background), Vacclav, 33 (top), Rudolf Tepfenhart, 34, Jeremy Richards, 38,
Zaptik, 39 (bottom left); TOTO USA, Inc.: 42; Wikipedia: Lobsterthermidor, 20 (top), 45 (bottom);
York Archaeological Trust: 17 (top).

Printed in the United States of America in Melrose Park, Illinois.
032011   006112LKF11

TABLE OF CONTENTS

Chapter 1

The Seat of Life

The average person spends about three years sitting on one. The most expensive one costs about $19 million. Holy Roman Emperor Charles V was born on one in the 1500s. Elvis Presley died on one. What are we talking about? Toilets, of course!

Civilizations have been judged by the quality of their toilets. People in the first permanent communities had to find clean ways of relieving themselves. From pits to pots, a society can often be judged by where citizens put their waste.

Come take a look at the long, fascinating history of the toilet. From its beginnings to toilets of the future, we'll leave no bowl unflushed. Grab rubber gloves and a scrub brush. Let's plunge into the world of toilets!

civilization—an organized and advanced society

SERIOUS ABOUT TOILETS

Did you know that toilets save lives? Clean waste removal and proper sanitation have improved human health more than any other invention in history. Unfortunately, 40 percent of the world's people don't have proper waste removal facilities. More than 2 million people die each year because of illnesses from poor sanitation.

The World Toilet Organization (WTO) was founded in 2001. It works to improve sanitation conditions. The WTO helps the 2.5 billion people who don't have clean waste removal facilities.

The WTO set up the World Toilet College. The organization teaches toilet design and maintenance, as well as sanitation technologies. The WTO named November 19 World Toilet Day to focus on the importance of toilets.

People participating in World Toilet Day

FACT:

One event of World Toilet Day is "The Big Squat." People around the world squat for one minute to remind others of the importance of toilets!

Chapter 2

Really Roughing It

The earliest humans relieved themselves wherever they were. They probably just left their waste on the ground. Maybe they covered it with dirt or buried it. Eventually, they had to solve how to get rid of their waste.

ancient indoor toilet

Taking It Indoors

The oldest indoor toilet was discovered in the Orkney Islands off the northern coast of Scotland. The stone huts that housed toilets date back about 5,000 years. People relieved themselves in hollows along the walls of the huts. The hollows were connected to a drain. The waste drained into an underground sewer system.

Sumerian Sanitation

About 5,000 years ago, the Sumerians ruled the area once known as Mesopotamia. Today this area is the country of Iraq. Sumerians built toilets in many of the houses in the city of Babylon. Each toilet was an opening in the floor of a room. Underneath the opening was a hole in the ground to hold waste. This hole was called a cesspit. People squatted over the hole to relieve themselves. This is called an Eastern-style toilet.

modern Eastern-style toilet

Have a Seat!

Mesopotamian ruler Sargon II built a palace with 300 rooms. He included six toilets. In these toilets, a seat was placed above the cesspit. This is called a Western-style toilet. The user poured water into the cesspit to flush away the waste.

Down in the Valley

brick-lined sewer system in Mohenjo-daro

The Harappans built the city of Mohenjo-daro about 4,600 years ago. The city was built along the Indus River Valley in present-day Pakistan. It featured an amazing system of waste removal.

The city was made up of neat rows of brick houses. Brick-lined sewers ran along the sides of the streets. These sewers were connected to each house by an open brick-lined gutter. Both Eastern-style and Western-style toilets were used. The waste dropped into a drain, then into the gutter, and then flowed to the sewer. The city's sewer system emptied into a large cesspit. The cesspit was cleaned out by city workers.

Great Pyramids, Terrible Toilets

The ancient Egyptians (about 3150 BC to 31 BC) are famous for building pyramids. But when it came to toilet technology, they were the pits. The best ancient Egyptian toilet was found in the city of Tel el-Amarna. They placed a toilet seat over a compartment containing sand. The seat was made from wood, clay, or limestone. It was smooth and had a hole in the middle. Servants cleaned and changed the sand under the toilet seat.

ancient limestone toilet seat

papyrus grass

FACT:

The Roll of Toilet Paper

The ancient Egyptians made toilet paper from papyrus grass. They also used it to make writing paper and scrolls.

The First Flushers of Crete

The mythical Minotaur was said to live in King Minos' maze.

Crete is an island 60 miles (97 km) southeast of mainland Greece. About 3,000 years ago, King Minos built an amazing palace in the city of Knossos. It had more than 1,400 rooms. It also had a mind-boggling maze inside. A remarkable discovery in the queen's quarters earns the palace its place in this book. The queen had a flush toilet! The toilet had a wooden seat and a pan. Moving water flushed the contents of the pan through a system of pipes and drains. This system was connected to sewers. Water flowed to the palace through clay pipes.

Taking It **PUBLIC**

The ancient Greeks were the first to build public latrines. They were used by more than one person at a time. One latrine had marble benches. There were four holes, and it could be used by four people at one time. A ditch near the users' feet carried running water to flush away the waste.

Chamber Pots

Many Greeks used chamber pots to relieve themselves. Chamber pots are bowls with handles. They were usually kept near a bed or in a cabinet. Historians believe the wealthy people of Sybaris, Greece, invented the chamber pot. They were said to be too lazy to leave a room to relieve themselves!

ancient Greek child's potty

FACT:
The words "potty," "potty training," and "potty seat" come from the term *chamber pot*.

The Waters of Rome

Several ancient civilizations used sewers and water to get rid of human waste. The ancient Romans did it on a grand scale. Their accomplishments changed the course of toilet history.

This sewer is part of the Cloaca Maxima.

The Cloaca Maxima

The Etruscans lived in central Italy from about 800 BC to 500 BC. The Roman Empire eventually took them over. The Etruscans built the ancient world's finest sewer system, the Cloaca Maxima. It drained excess water and waste into the Tiber River. Parts of this system are still in use today.

Water, Water, Everywhere!

The Romans built **aqueducts** under and above the ground to bring water into Rome from miles away. The water was used in fountains and public baths. It was also used in government buildings and some private homes.

ancient public restroom

The Romans had plenty of running water and a sewer system in place. Next, they built public restrooms throughout the city. The restrooms were usually built over a channel of running water. Users sat on a stone seat with a hole in the center. A bucket containing salt water was placed next to each latrine. In it was a long stick with a sponge at one end. People used the spongy end to wipe their bottoms. Now you know where the phrase, "Getting hold of the wrong end of the stick" comes from!

aqueduct—a structure for carrying flowing water

A Night Out on the Town Latrine

Romans paid a small fee to use public latrines. People gathered there to relax, use the toilets, and chat with neighbors. Some of these public latrines were simple. Others were fancy. The latrine at Ostia had marble toilet seats and beautiful mosaics. It also had carved dolphins to separate the multiple seats for privacy.

WATCH OUT BELOW!

Even with a system to deliver running water, most Romans used chamber pots or cesspits. Many Romans simply emptied the contents of their chamber pots out their windows. Sometimes people walking by were dumped on. Fortunately, a law allowed the victims of the soakings to take the dumper to court. The courts often forced the dumper to pay money to the person who was hit by the falling waste.

The Roman Empire

- Atlantic Ocean
- Britain
- Gaul
- Italy
- Rome
- Spain
- Macedonia
- Black Sea
- Caspian Sea
- Greece
- ASIA MINOR
- Cyprus
- Crete
- Syria
- Judea
- Jerusalem
- Mediterranean Sea
- AFRICA
- Egypt
- Nile River
- Red Sea

☐ Roman Empire

The End of an Era

The Romans spread their sanitation technology throughout their empire. But as the Romans came under attack by fierce tribes from across Europe, the Roman Empire crumbled. Europe was dragged into a period of 1,000 years in which many things about sanitation and toilet technology were forgotten.

ruins of latrines at an ancient Roman fort in England

Chapter 3

Roughing It

Turning Back Progress

The tribes that overran the Roman Empire destroyed many aqueducts and public latrines. These tribes then used more primitive forms of toilet technology. Germanic tribes of the 300s often dug pits for storage. Then they put their poop on top. This discouraged invaders from looting the valuables. The Celts of the British Isles dug pits around their huts. The pits were used to bury their waste and garbage.

invaders destroy a Roman city

Middle Ages Misery

The period from about AD 500 to AD 1500 is known as the Middle Ages. Most of Europe was filthy and unhealthy during that time. The muddy streets were filled with garbage, human waste, and rotting bodies of dead animals. The filth helped spread a series of epidemics. The Black Death epidemic happened in the mid-1300s. More than 75 million people died from the bubonic plague.

epidemic—the quick spread of a disease through a population

A VALUABLE DISCOVERY

Andrew Jones is a researcher from the University of York in England. He found a 1,000-year-old piece of Viking poop. It is on display at the Archaeological Resource Centre in York. It is believed to be the largest human fossil poop ever found. It measures 8 inches (20 cm) long by 2 inches (5 cm) wide.

fossilized Viking poop

FACT:

Some toilet facilities, called loos, were built during the Middle Ages. Dick Whittington's Long House was a public loo. It could be used by 64 men and 64 women at one time. The facility was built on London Bridge. The waste was dumped directly into the Thames River.

London Bridge was completed in 1209.

A Long Drop

What were latrines like inside the castles and towns of the Middle Ages? European castles and buildings had closets called garderobes. They were small seats that were often made of stone. These seats were built into hollows in walls. The waste dropped many feet into a stream, moat, pit, or barrel.

The men who cleaned up and removed the waste were called nightmen because they worked in the evening. Nightmen were paid high wages for their services. They often made even more money by selling the waste to farmers who used it as fertilizer.

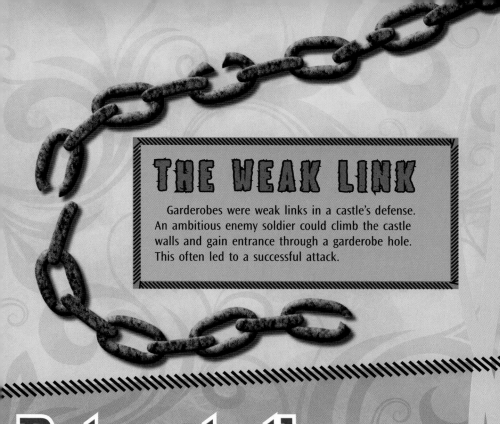

Garderobes were weak links in a castle's defense. An ambitious enemy soldier could climb the castle walls and gain entrance through a garderobe hole. This often led to a successful attack.

Return to the Chamber Pot

Not everyone had a garderobe or even a latrine during the Middle Ages. Most people still used chamber pots. Medieval chamber pots were usually made from earthenware, tin, or copper. They had a wide bottom and an opening with a narrow neck.

By the 1700s wealthy people were having their chamber pots made of fine Chinese porcelain. These fancy chamber pots were often decorated with hand-painted art.

Sitting Pretty

A new form of toilet, called the closestool, became popular during the 1500s. It was a chamber pot in a fancy box. The chamber pot could be removed for cleaning. Each box had a hinged top and padded seat for the user to sit on. The padded seat was often covered in velvet or leather. The boxes were elegantly decorated with gold, silver, and engravings of birds and landscapes. Owners often displayed their closestools as handsome pieces of furniture.

FACT:

King Louis XIV of France (1638–1715) had 264 closestools at Versailles. He even greeted visitors while using his favorite closestool!

Father of the Modern Toilet

Englishman Sir John Harington introduced the Ajax in 1596. The Ajax was the first toilet with mechanical parts. A tank filled with water was flushed to let its contents out. The water flowed down a pipe and into the bowl to clean out the waste. Sir John introduced his invention in a book full of toilet jokes. The book offended many people. His godmother, Queen Elizabeth, even banished him from her royal court. But she eventually forgave him and allowed Harington to install an Ajax at Richmond Palace.

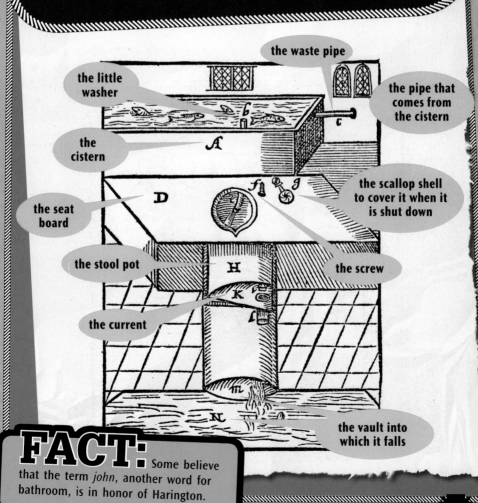

the waste pipe

the little washer

the pipe that comes from the cistern

the cistern

the scallop shell to cover it when it is shut down

the seat board

the stool pot

the screw

the current

the vault into which it falls

FACT: Some believe that the term *john*, another word for bathroom, is in honor of Harington.

Old Habits Die Hard

European immigrants coming to the United States in the 1600s brought their toilet habits with them. For many settlers, the wilderness was their bathroom. Others used chamber pots and emptied them into the streets. American settlers also created a new type of loo—the outhouse. Outhouses were small wooden buildings that held a bench with a hole in it. A deep pit or bucket was under the hole. This setup was similar to privies of the past, but building the outhouse away from the home kept the smell at bay. Some people decorated the walls of their outhouses with poems, graffiti, or wallpaper.

The Privacy of the Privy

Back in Europe, privies were beginning to catch on. Instead of just a hole in the ground, these privies were closets with a chamber pot or closestool inside. For those who could afford them, the privy offered privacy.

THE WATER CLOSET

The water closet was introduced in Europe in the 1700s. It was a privy with a flushing toilet. A user pulled on a handle to let water from an overhead tank into the toilet. In its early form, the bowl and the pipes that carried the waste away were not blocked off from each other. This caused quite a stink in European homes.

In 1775 Alexander Cummings came to the rescue. He designed a toilet that included an S-valve. This kept a certain amount of standing water in the pipe. The water blocked odors from coming back up into the bowl and smelling up the owner's home.

FACT:

During the 1700s, royalty used goose feathers to wipe themselves after using the toilet.

The Great Stink

By the 1800s many major cities still had serious waste problems. In the summer of 1858, London experienced The Great Stink. For years human waste and decaying garbage had been draining into nearby rivers. Hot summer temperatures caused germs to grow out of control. They created an awful smell. Thousands of people died after getting sick from the germs. Heavy rains finally ended the heat, and the stinky smell passed. Londoners didn't want to live through that stench again. They built more efficient sewers and better water supply systems.

London, England

Sewers to be Proud of

Eventually the sewer systems of cities throughout Europe and the United States were improved. Citizens of Paris were so proud of their expanding sewer system that it became a tourist attraction. Passengers traveled through the underground tunnels in wagons or boats.

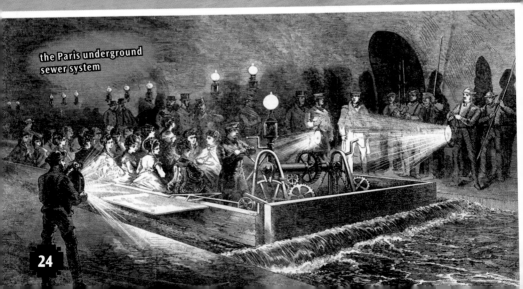

the Paris underground sewer system

A Bold New Future

Inventions in the 1800s paved the way for a healthier, cleaner way of life.

1885

Thomas Crapper designed a new flush toilet. Water automatically refilled the tank better than earlier designs.

1884

Thomas Twyford introduced the porcelain toilet bowl. Porcelain bowls were easier to clean than bowls made of other materials.

George Jennings designed a device that increased the pressure of water entering the toilet. This allowed for a better cleaning of the bowl.

1852

CRAPPER'S
VALVELESS WASTE PREVENTER
N° 814.

a Thomas Crapper & Company toilet tank

FACT:

Paris has more than 1,300 miles (2,090 km) of sewer tunnels. You can visit the Paris Sewers Museum to learn more about them. The museum is located in a sewer!

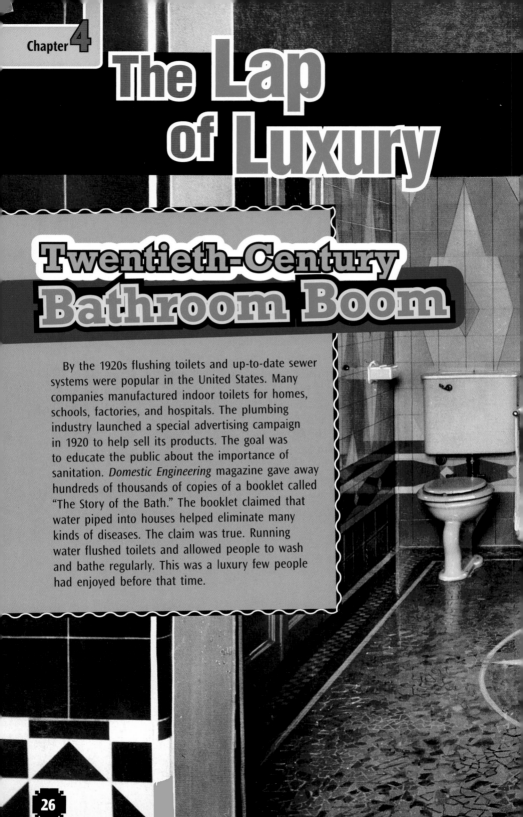

Chapter 4

The Lap of Luxury

Twentieth-Century Bathroom Boom

By the 1920s flushing toilets and up-to-date sewer systems were popular in the United States. Many companies manufactured indoor toilets for homes, schools, factories, and hospitals. The plumbing industry launched a special advertising campaign in 1920 to help sell its products. The goal was to educate the public about the importance of sanitation. *Domestic Engineering* magazine gave away hundreds of thousands of copies of a booklet called "The Story of the Bath." The booklet claimed that water piped into houses helped eliminate many kinds of diseases. The claim was true. Running water flushed toilets and allowed people to wash and bathe regularly. This was a luxury few people had enjoyed before that time.

20th-century bathroom

Japanese Innovation

Japanese inventors have recently come up with new toilet concepts. For $1,100 your toilet rinses your bottom and gently dries it too! It also has an automatic lid that opens and closes when you enter or exit the room.

If you don't like being alone in the bathroom, try the Ladybug bathroom attendant. Why? The Ladybug talks to you while you're taking care of business. This robot helper also has water storage units and scrub brushes to help keep your bathroom sparkling clean. For $30,000 you can have a spotless bathroom and great conversation!

Urinals for Women

Some women are afraid of catching diseases from sitting on toilet seats. Instead of sitting, they stand over toilets and urinate. In the 1950s American Standard produced the Sanistand line of female urinals. They never really caught on, and the company stopped manufacturing the urinals in the 1970s. The truth is that it is very unlikely to get a disease from a toilet seat. It is more important to wash your hands thoroughly after using the bathroom. You are more likely to transfer germs from your hands to your nose or your mouth. These are more common entry points for germs than the skin on your bottom.

urinal—a kind of toilet that a user stands over and urinates into

iPod
Music
Photos
Videos
Extras
Settings
Shuffle Songs
Now Playing

MENU

iCarta

Attention,
Music Lovers!

Do you like to rock out and wipe up at the same time? Then the iPod toilet roll holder is for you. It has a built-in docking station, four speakers, and a dispenser for your toilet paper. The price tag on this hi-tech gizmo is about $230.

Toilets in Space

Astronauts aboard the International Space Station (ISS) use a toilet called the waste collection system. The system includes a toilet, urinal, and odor and bacteria filters. The urinal can be used by both men and women. Solid waste is collected in a container and dried for in-flight storage. Liquid waste is sent into space. This system isn't cheap. In 2007 the United States bought an ISS toilet system from Russia for $19 million!

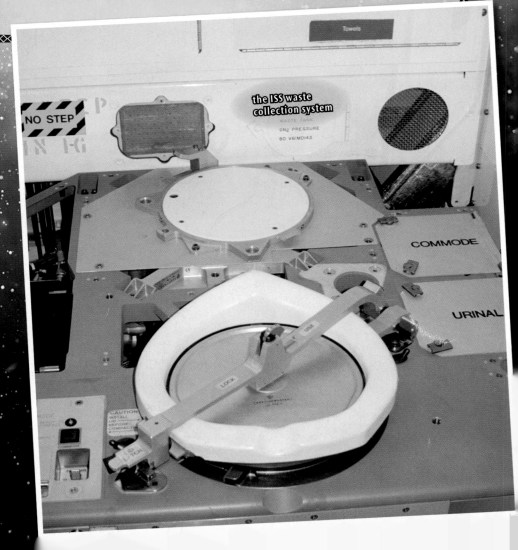

the ISS waste collection system

Toilets in the Big Apple

Do you know about self-cleaning public toilets? After the user leaves the bathroom, a robotic arm swings out over the toilet and sprays it with cleaner. Jets spray cleansers across the floor and sink. Then dryers blow hot air over everything. In 2001 these self-cleaning toilets were installed in small buildings on some streets in New York City.

New Yorkers liked the new idea at first. But they soon stopped using the toilets. Why? People claimed the self-cleaning devices weren't as sanitary as cleaning by hand. Eventually all the self-cleaning toilets were removed. They were replaced by toilets that are cleaned 15 to 20 times a day by people.

GOING GREEN

Compost toilets are often used where water is in short supply, such as on boats, at campsites, and at construction sites. Besides saving water, compost toilets break down the bacteria in waste that can cause disease. They also break down human waste into humus, which can be buried around tree roots and nonedible plants as fertilizer.

Treating Sewage Kindly

Wastewater is used water. It contains human waste, food scraps, soaps, and chemicals. In the late 1900s, cities began using filters and chemicals to treat wastewater before it was returned to lakes and rivers. Later different kinds of bacteria were added to treat the water. Today sewage is treated several times in most modern cities. During the process liquid waste is separated from solid waste, bacteria is added, and filters are often used. Solid waste is burned or used on farms as fertilizer. Liquid waste is treated with chemicals and returned to lakes and rivers.

The White House is home to 35 bathrooms.

Toilet Tidbits

- In the United States more toilets are flushed during halftime of the Super Bowl than at any other time of the year.
- In 2007 19 percent of homes in Afghanistan had TVs, but only 7 percent had flush toilets.
- The White House has 35 bathrooms.
- The Pentagon uses about 660 rolls of toilet paper each day.

wastewater treatment plant

Chapter 5
Toilet Customs Around the World

The Hindu Brahmins

Brahmin priests of the Hindu religion follow strict guidelines when relieving themselves. The priest carries a pot filled with water to a clean place. He removes his slippers, covers his head with a piece of clothing, and stoops low to the ground. He must not look at the sun, moon, stars, or a sacred temple. He must also remain silent. After finishing, he carefully washes himself. Then he must wash and rinse his mouth eight times.

a Hindu temple in Delhi, India

the Great Exhibition of 1851

Useful Urine

Throughout history urine has been used for many purposes. Here are a few of the most memorable:

- In ancient Roman times, the Gauls used urine to whiten their teeth.
- Pop star Madonna urinates on her feet to cure athlete's foot.
- Former baseball star Moises Alou put urine on his hands to soften his calluses.

Madonna

Keeping It Tidy

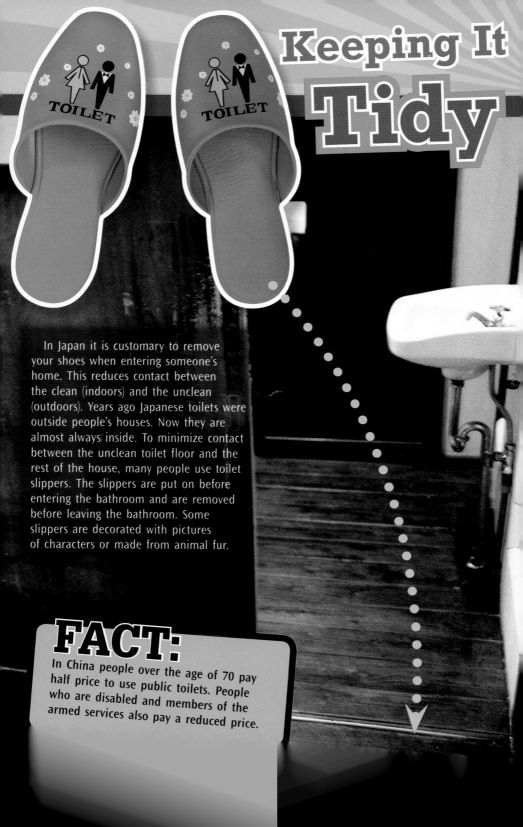

In Japan it is customary to remove your shoes when entering someone's home. This reduces contact between the clean (indoors) and the unclean (outdoors). Years ago Japanese toilets were outside people's houses. Now they are almost always inside. To minimize contact between the unclean toilet floor and the rest of the house, many people use toilet slippers. The slippers are put on before entering the bathroom and are removed before leaving the bathroom. Some slippers are decorated with pictures of characters or made from animal fur.

FACT:

In China people over the age of 70 pay half price to use public toilets. People who are disabled and members of the armed services also pay a reduced price.

mixing a love potion

Functional Feces

Over the years people have found creative and unusual ways to use human waste.

- In ancient Rome urine was collected and used in the process of making leather from animal skins.
- In the Middle Ages, women used feces to make love potions. They believed the potions would make a man fall in love.
- Hundreds of years ago, tribal women in Australia put human feces on their heads. They did this to show their sorrow when mourning the death of a loved one.

People in Need of Potties

India is a rapidly growing nation. Its leaders haven't yet found a way to deal with the amount of human waste the nation produces. Wealthy people in Indian cities often have toilets such as those used in the United States and other Western countries. Flushing squat toilets are also used.

Yet less than 30 percent of India's people have bathrooms or access to public toilets. People in urban slums often have no running water. They relieve themselves along roadsides, in rivers, on farmlands, or in public parks. Some use a bucket placed in a hut.

Only a few Indian cities and towns have sewer systems. Many of these systems do not have waste treatment plants. Poor sanitation is the leading cause of disease in the nation.

An Unforgettable Dining Experience

The Modern Toilet Restaurant in Taiwan is a toilet-themed restaurant chain. The seats are made from toilet bowls with images of roses, seashells, or famous paintings. Customers eat from bowls shaped like toilets or bathtubs. They sip their drinks from urinal-shaped cups.

FACT:

According to a United Nations report, more people in India have access to a cell phone than to a toilet.

Chapter 6

Future Flushes

Go With the Flo!

Toilet designers at Arizona State University have created a device that might soon be in our homes. It's called the Flo. This toilet functions like a squat toilet. Using the Flo has been compared to doing yoga exercises because you strengthen your stomach and back muscles while you use it. The Flo uses less water to flush than a standard toilet. It also reuses water from hand washing. Plus, it's a totally hands-off operation—the Flo flushes itself!

WHEN SPACE IS TIGHT

For those who live in small places, there's the Washup. It combines a toilet and a washing machine. You can use the toilet and do your laundry at the same time! The washer is located on a wall behind the toilet. The Washup is a great water-saving device. The water used in the washer is reused to flush the toilet.

The All-in-One Toilet

The futuristic Home Core toilet combines a toilet bowl, sink, pop-up mirror, and table. Its design saves water. The water used to wash your hands is stored in a tank and used when you flush the toilet. The device is a great space-saver. Each part of the Home Core folds up or swivels out from a single unit. What's the most unusual part of the Home Core? It has a coffee warmer built into the back!

Tops in Toilet Technology!

The employees of TOTO, a toilet and plumbing manufacturing company, are among the world leaders in toilet design. One of the company's recent products has a control panel with a number of buttons on it. The user presses one button for a heavy-duty flush or a different button for a less powerful blast. Pressing other buttons lowers and raises the toilet seat, washes the user with a stream of water, and even blow dries the user's bottom!

Another product, called the Washlet, might be the most elegant toilet ever designed. A remote-control device operates a washing wand, a heated seat, and a deodorizer. The Washlet also has a "tornado flush" feature.

Washlet toilet

TURN THE PAGE

Czech designer Jan Ctvrtnik has a solution to sharing the family toilet bowl—personal toilet seats. Called the Toilet Pages, the design allows each person to have his or her own "page," or seat. Handy tabs stick out on the side of each page. Family members can quickly flip to their own comfy seats.

The ovens used to make toilet bowls are called kilns.

FACT:

The standard toilet bowl is made from clay that is covered with a shiny glaze. To dry and harden the glazed clay, it is baked in a special oven at temperatures up to 2,200° Fahrenheit (1,200° Celsius).

The Last Scoop

People have made a lot of progress in dealing with their waste since the time they first found relief in the outdoors. Throughout the centuries many people have played important roles in advancing the technology of the toilet. Some were serious builders and inventors. Others entertained us with their zany and silly solutions to handling waste. Let's hope the future of toilets is as exciting as the past has been.

An early sewer system is constructed in Mohenjo-daro.

2600 BC

Garderobes are used in castles of the Middle Ages.

AD 500–1500

3000 BC

The earliest known toilets are built in the Orkney Islands, Crete, and Babylon.

312 BC

The Romans begin building advanced plumbing systems and aqueducts.

Improved sanitation systems and waste disposal methods are created worldwide.

1900s

The Great Stink strikes London.

1858

1884

Thomas Crapper invents an improved flush system.

The water closet becomes a popular form of toilet.

1700s

Sir John Harington invents the first toilet with working parts.

1596

Early 1500s

Closestools become popular.

GLOSSARY

aqueduct (AK-wuh-duhkt)—a structure for carrying flowing water

bacteria (bak-TEER-ee-uh)—microscopic living organisms that can cause disease

civilization (si-vuh-luh-ZAY-shuhn)—an organized and advanced society

epidemic (ep-uh-DE-mik)—the quick spread of a disease through a population

sanitation (san-uh-TAY-shuhn)—methods of ensuring a clean water supply and getting rid of sewage

urinal (YOOR-uhn-uhl)—a kind of toilet that a user stands over and urinates into

urine (YOOR-uhn)—liquid human or animal waste

valve (VALV)—a movable part that controls the flow of liquids or gases through a pipe

READ MORE

Harper, Charise Mericle. *Flush!: The Scoop on Poop Throughout the Ages.* New York: Little Brown, 2007.

Miller, Connie Colwell. *Getting to Know Your Toilet: The Disgusting Story Behind Your Home's Strangest Feature.* Mankato, Minn.: Capstone Press, 2009.

Raum, Elizabeth. *The Story Behind Toilets.* Chicago , Ill.: Heinemann Library, 2009.

INTERNET SITES

FactHound offers a safe, fun way to find Internet sites related to this book. All of the sites on FactHound have been researched by our staff.

Here's all you do:

Visit *www.facthound.com*

Type in this code: 9781429654890

INDEX